ꘓꗋ ꘐꗏ ꗧꖁ

ꖁꖬ ꗪꗏ

HMONG ALPHABET

Level 2

ꘓꘀ ꗧꗑꘉ

HMONG
MULTIMEDIA

Hmong Alphabet: Level 2
Copyright © 2014 Hmong Multimedia
hmongmultimedia@gmail.com

ꓳꞺ ꞽꓮꙶ ꓟꞺ 2009 ꓸꖹꓵ�699ꓸꙶ ꓟ ꙶ9ꖹ Ꙇ�50ꓔꙺ ꞽꞡ ꖽꞺ ꙶ�

Author: Chia Koua Vang

ၵၢၼ် တၢင်း

ၵၢၼ် တၢင်း					ၼႃႈ

ႁႃႊ

<u>ႁႃႊ ၵၢႈ</u>　　　　　<u>ႁႃႊ ၸၢႈ</u>

ꩳ　　　　　　　　ꩡ

ꧥ　　　　　　　ꩭ

ꧠ　　　　　　　ꧨ

ꩱ　　　　　　　ꩢ

ꧦ　　　　　　　ꧣ

ꩤ　　　　　　ꩬ

ꧪ　　　　　　ꧫ

ꩮ　　　　　　ꩯ

ꩡ　　　　　　ꩧ

ꩲ　　　　　　ꩠ

ꩶ　　　　　　ꩳ

ᤔᤡᤖ

R
K
Ш
Γ
Ц
A
C
Ш
Ǝ
A
♄
Ч

ปๆ

ⴾ
ⴼ
ⴼ
Ɱ
Ⴀ
Ⴁ
Ⴄ

ㅿ️Ꝥ

●   ㅿ️Ꝥ ㄸㅞ

▼   ㅿ️Ꝥ ㅄㅞ

▬   ㅿ️Ꝥ ㅕ

●●   ㅿ️Ꝥ ㅂㅞ

▼   ㅿ️Ꝥ ㅁㅠ

ᜫᜩ ᜦᜮᜢ ᜧᜦ

ဗီဟဆိႝ်ဏြ

R Ṙ Řّ

K Ǩ Ǩّ

ш ш̇ ш̌

ᴜ ᴜ̇ ᴜ̌

∀ ∀̇ ∀̌

ᴄ ᴄ̇ ᴄ̌

m m̈ m̈

ᴚ ᴚ̇ ᴚ̌

A Å Ǎ

Ⴌ Ⴌ̇ Ⴌ̌

Ч Ч̇ Ч̌

ຫ ຫ ຫ

ຍ ຍ ຍ

ທ ທ ທ

ຄ ຄ ຄ

ຍ ຍ ຍ

ຍ ຍ ຍ

ႮꞐꞐႨꞐ̃ Ꞑ

R

ႮR

Ⴎ   R =   ႮR

ႮR, ꞐR, ∩R, Ꞑ̄R, ꞐR, Ꞑ̃R. ႮRꞐ̄꞊,
ႮRꞐꞌ, ႮRꞐ̄ꞌ, ႮRꞐꞌꞌ, ႮR∩ꞌ.
ꞐRꞌRꞐRꞐꞌ Ꞑ̃꞊ႮR. ꞐRꞌRꞐ̃꞊
ႮRꞐRꞐ.

Ṙ

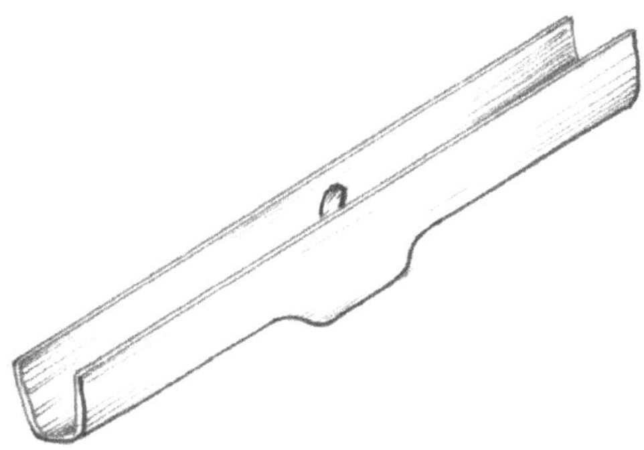

ṅṘ

ṅ Ṙ = ṅṘ

ṅṘ, ʎṘ, ƏṘ, ṅṘ, ṅṘ. ƏʉṅṘ ЛѶ, ṅṘ ෆṅ Л. ʎṘ ṅṘ ෆṅ ЛʋṘħ. ЫR ʎR ṅṘħ. ЫR ʎṅ ṅṘ ෆṅ ЛෆЗ ʎȦ ƏṘ. ЫR ʎR ЛЗ ʎR ෆRħ.

Ⱶ Ř̌

Ⱶ Ř = Ⱶ Ř̌

Ⱶ Ř̌, Ꞇ Ř̌, Ʌ Ř̌, ∩̄ Ř̌, ⱳ̇ Ř̌, ꙍ Ř̌, ∩̄ Ř̌. Ⱶ Ř̌
∩̄ Ř̌, Ⱶ Ř̌ Ⱨ Ă̌, Ⱶ Ř̌ ꙍ Ɐ, Ⱶ Ř̌ Ʌ ᶆ, Ⱶ Ř̌ ш ⱳ̇.
ᴖ ᶆ̇ ᴂᴚ Ⱶ Ř̌ ∩̄ Ř̌ ⱳ̇ Ř̌ ħ. ∩ ⱷ̇ ᶆ̇ Ꞇ Ř̌ ꙅ ш ᵿ ᴛ
ꞷ Ř̌ ħ. ᴕᴚ ⱷ̇ Ř̌ ∩̄ᴚ Ʌ ȧ ∩̄ ⱴ̌ ᵿ̇ ᴕ Ⱶ Ř̌.

K

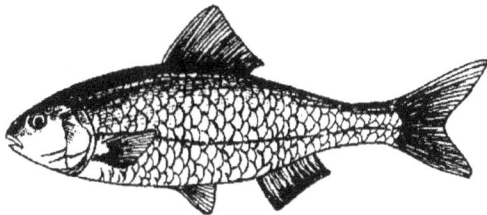

Ħ̄K

Ħ̄ K = Ħ̄K

Ħ̄K, ⌀K, ⍟K, ∨K, ∏K, ⋏K, ᕙK.
∩Ⅎ̈Ħ̄K�, ∩⌀KⱮKĦ̄K. Ħ̄K⍊Ⅎ̌
ᴔℲ̈ᕙᖚᗺᵻᴔⅎ̈. Ħ̄K⍊Ⅎ̌ᕐᵻH∀ᵻᗕ
Ⅎ̈Ⅎ̌. ᖚᵱᵻᴕ∩RᵻᴿĦ̄K⍊Ⅎ̌ᴔⅎ̈ᵰ
ᕙᵱᗺᵻᴔⅎ̈.

K̇

ᑌHK̇

ᑌH K̇ = ᑌHK̇

ᑌHK̇, ᑌ̇HK̇, ᑌK̇, ᑌ̇K̇, ᐱ̇K̇, ᗰK̇, ᗰ̄K̇, ᗰ̈K̇.
ᗩᘖ ᑌHK̇, ᑌHK̇ ᗯᑫ, ᑌHK̇ ᗩᗄ, ᑌHK̇ ᗱṀᗯ,
ᑌHK̇ ᒍᑌ. ᑌHK̇ ᑎK̇ᕼ, ᑌHK̇ ᑎK̇ ᗰᘖ ᑌHK̇.
ᗰȦ ᗰᘖ ᘖᘓ ᗰK̇ ᗰR ᐱȦ ᗩᘖ ᑌHK̇ ᗯᑫ.
ᑕK̇ ᗩR ᘖᗄ ᑌHK̇, ᑌHK̇ ᑌᗄᕼ ᑕK̇.

ᒼꓘ

ᗷᒼꓘ = ᗷᒼꓘ

ᗷᒼꓘ, ᒐᒼꓘ, ꓪᒼꓘ, ꓦᒼꓘ, ꒼ꓘ, ᒄᒼꓘ, ᒐᒼꓘ, ᒼꓘ.

ꓦᗷᒼꓘᒐᒼ ꓦ꒐, ᗷᒼꓘ ꓦ꒐ ꓦᒼ. ꒕꒼꒼
ᒐᒼ꒐꒐꒼, ᗷᒼ꒐꒐ᒐR ᒐᒼ ꓦᗷᒼꓘ ꓦ꒐
ꓦᒼ. ᗷᒼᒐᒐR ᒐᒼ ꓦᗷᒼꓘᒐᒼ ꓦ꒐.

วิพ

วิ   พ = วิพ

วิพ, ก่พ, งพ, ตพ, บิพ, บาพ, ธพ, บพ,
งพ. กิว้ วิพ, วิพ กก้ ณว้, วิพ กก้ ธิR.
ยก้ ณิR ก่ ก้ กิว้ วิพ. ยก้ ก ว้ วิพ หง
กก้ ติง บิกฏ บิง ผ่ ฟ่ ฟ่ก่ ฆ ว้ ฟ่ฆ.

ᘔᘁ

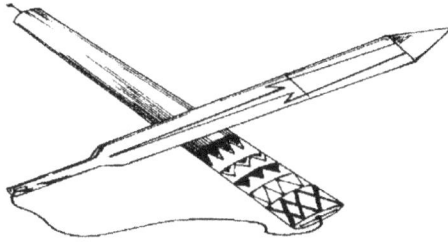

ᘎᘁᘳ

ᘎ   ᘁᘳ = ᘎᘁᘳ

ᘎᘁᘳ, ᘀᘁᘳ, ᘍᘁᘳ, ᘂᘁᘳ, ᘄᘁᘳ, ᘅᘁᘳ, ᘆᘁᘳ, ᘇᘁᘳ, ᘈᘁᘳ. ᘉᘊ ᘎᘁᘳ ᘋᘌ ᘍᘎ, ᘎᘁᘳ ᘏᘌ ᘐᘑ, ᘉᘊ ᘎᘁᘳ ᘒR ᘓᘔ ᘕᘖ ᘗᘘ, ᘙᘚ ᘛR ᘜR ᘝᘞ ᘉᘊ ᘎᘁᘳ ᘟᘠᘡ. ᘙᘚ ᘛR ᘢᘣ ᘤᘥ ᘦᘧ ᘎᘁᘳ ᘟᘠᘡ.

21

ፓ ፖ = ፓ ፖ

23

24

25

ᎦᎸᏫ

ᎠᎸᏫ

ᎠᎸ ᎦᎸ = ᎠᎸᏫ

ᎠᎸᏫ, ᎤᎸᏫ, ᎦᎸᏫ, ᎥᎸᏫ, ᏓᎸᏫ, ᎧᎸᏫ. ᏁᎠᎸᏫᎥᎠ,
ᏗᎠᎸᏫᏕᎯᎸᎢ. ᎣᎸᎡᏣᎠᎸᏫᎠᎳᎠᎣ. ᏁᎠᎸᏫ,
ᏗᎠᎸᏫ,ᎣᎸᎥᏫᎢᎸᎣᎷᎠᎡᏣᎠᎸᏫᎠᎳᎠᎣ,
ᎣᎸᎠᎸᏫᎤᎸᎠᏏᎷᎠᏏᎤᎦᎢ.

∀

ก่∀

ก่ ∀ = ก่∀

꒕

ꀍÅ

ꀍ Å = ꀍÅ

ꀍÅ, ꀎÅ, ꀥÅ, ꀕÅ, ꀱÅ, ꀨÅ, ꀫÅ, ꀬÅ.
ꀠꀍÅ, ꀍÅꀯÅ, ꀍÅꀫꀳ, ꀍÅ ꀴꀵ ꀲꀶ.
ꀍÅ ꀷꀸꀹꀺ ꀻꀺ ꀼ꒓ ꀽꀾ ꀍꀿ ꀠꁀ ꀍꁁ ꀲꁂ.
ꀠꁃꁄꁅ. ꀍÅ ꁆꁇ ꁈA ꁉꁊ ꁋ꒕ ꁌ꒓ ꁍꁎ.
ꁉꁊ ꁋ꒕ꀥÅꁏꀍÅ.

28

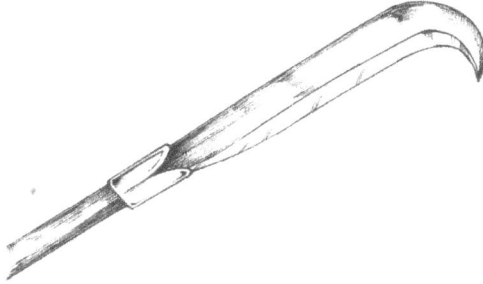

ꪝꪲꪀ꪿

ꪝꪲ ꪀ꪿ = ꪝꪲꪀ꪿

ꪝꪲꪀ꪿, ꪹꪎꪀ꪿, ꪺꪀ꪿, ꪀꪀ꪿, ꪁꪀ꪿, ꪂꪀ꪿, ꪶꪉꪀ꪿, ꪫꪀ꪿,
ꪻꪀ꪿, ꪒꪀ꪿, ꪛꪀ꪿, ꪹꪘꪀ꪿, ꪹꪔꪀ꪿. ꪫꪻꪝꪲꪀ꪿, ꪝꪲꪀ꪿
ꪶꪙꪜꪥꪚ꫁, ꪝꪲꪀ꪿ꪹꪎꪱ꫁ꪻꪙ꫁,ꪝꪲꪀ꪿ꪶꪙRꪏ,ꪝꪲꪀ꪿ꪶꪙR
ꪻꪈ, ꪺꪝꪲꪀ꪿ꪼꪨꪥꪺꪻꪙ꫁. ꪫꪲꪒꪶꪙꪱꪶꪙꪝ꫁ꪮ꪿ꪫꪲꪝ꫁
ꪫRꪫꪥꪝꪲꪀ꪿ꪀRꪶꪙꪜꪥꪚ꫁ꪣꪰꪹꪎꪱ꫁ꪻꪙ꫁.

ᑕ

ᑎᑕ

ᑎ ᑕ = ᑎᑕ

ᑎᑕ, ᚺᑕ, ᔓᑕ, ᚗᑕ, ᙎᑕ, ᔓᑕ, ᗰᑕ, ᑗᑕ.
ᔓᚺᑎᑕ, ᑎᑕᗰᑕᚗᑕ, ᑎᑕᑎᑕᕐᙏ. ᑎᑕ
ᑎᖈᙎᑫ, ᑎᑕᑎᖈᐱᚆ. ᔓᑕᑎᖈᐱᚗᔓᚺᑎᑕ.
ᔓᑕᙏᗺᗰᚆᑗᑗᑎᖈᑎᕐᙏᗰᚗᑲᗺᗢᙏ.

ꆈ꒳ꂷ

ꆈ ꒳ ꆈ꒳

ꆈ꒳, ꃅ꒳, ꀘ꒳, ꄮ꒳, ꆈ꒳, ꀋ꒳, ꁦ꒳, ꄷ꒳.
ꇁꐚ ꆈ꒳, ꆈ꒳ꆅR ꌦꐚ, ꆈ꒳ꆅR ꏂꐚ, ꆈ꒳
ꆅR ꌺꀉ. ꇅꐕꀋꇬ ꆈ꒳ ꃅꀉ ꆈ꒳ ꈎꑘꆀꄉ.
ꆈ꒳ ꈎꑘꆀꄉ ꄮꐥꇅꄢꆀꄉ ꄽꑟꒉA, ꆈ꒳ ꏂꐙ
ꀍꊂꒉꐛ.

31

ጠ፟ፘ

ጠ ፟ፘ ጠ፟ፘ

ጠ፟ፘ, ዞ፟ፘ, ፀ፟ፘ, ጓ፟ፘ, ቄ፟ፘ, ሀ፟ፘ, ሉ፟ፘ, ፧፟ፘ.
ቦጠ፟ፘጓ, ፀጠ፟ፘዘ, ይ፟ጚጓ፟ፘኊ, ሠ፝ዪ፥ጓ፟ፘ
ፇ፟ፆ. ቦ፟ዕ፟ፙ፟ዸ፟ፘጠ፟ፘቫ ጓ፟ፘፇ፟ፘ. ቦፒፒ
ቫሀ ሉ፟ፘ፟ጢ፟ፙ፟ፊ፟ፙ. ዘ ጓ፟ፘኊ ቦ፝ R ፊ ኮ ፧፟፧፟.

m

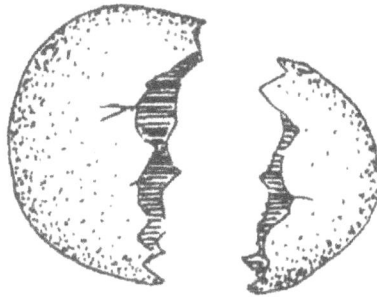

ᗡᙢ

ᗡ ᙢ ᗡᙢ

ሸ

ጺሸ

ጺ ሸ = ጺሸ

ጺሸ, ሀሸ, ሰሸ, ጠሸ, ገሸ, ፙሸ, ጸሸ, ሧሸ,
ቨሧ ጺሸ ዐ ጠR, ጺሸ ጠRሰሸ. ጺሸ ዾ ኧ
ጠ ጠሧ ዩ ጸ ሧኽ. ሀሸ ቨሧ ጺሸ ቨR ዾሧ
ሀሸ. ጺሸ ዐ ዸ, ጺሸ ሠ ጸ ዸ ዥ ዕ ዸ ወሸ.

လၢ့

ဃ့ၢ်

ဃ ၢ့် = ဃ့ၢ်

ဖၢ့်, တၢ့်, ၁ၢ့်, ၇ၢ့်, ၁့ၢ်, ဝှၢ့်, ၁ၢ့်, ၆ၢ့်,
ဖ့ၢ်, ဟၢ့်. ကဃ့ၢ် ဃ့ၢ်, ဃ့ၢ်ဖၢဟ ဖၢ့်, ဃ့ၢ်ဖ့ၢ်
ဟဲ့ၢ်. လၢ်ဟၤ ဃ့ၢ် ဖဟ ၇ၢ့်ဖၢဟ ဖၢ့်.
ဖ့ၢ်ဟဲ့ၢ်, ဃ့ၢ်ဟဃကR ၄ ၢ်တဟ. ၁ၢ့် ၢ်Rဃၢ
ကRဖဲ့ၢ် ဃ့ၢ်. ဃ့ၢ်ဟဃဖၢ့်ဖ့ၢ်.

ꤢ

ထိꤢ

ထိ ꤢ = ထိꤢ

ထိꤢ, ꤔိꤢ, ꤜꤢ, ꤘ̈ꤢ, ꤞ̇ꤢ, ဟꤢ, ꤘꤢ, ꤔꤢ,
ꤑꤜ̈ꤔ ထိꤢꤖꤛ, ထိꤢꤘꤢ̈, ထိꤢꤖꤛꤜꤛ̈ꤖꤛꤜꤛꤟ.
ꤔꤢ̈ꤘꤢꤟ ꤜꤛ̈ꤟꤟ ꤖꤛ̇ꤞR ꤜꤢ̇ ꤑꤜ̈ ထိꤢ
ꤖꤛꤜꤜ̈ꤖꤛꤑꤜ̈ꤜꤛꤥꤟꤑR ꤘꤢꤝꤘꤢ̈ ꤜꤜ̈.

36

ၸံ

ႜၸံ

ႜ ၸံ = ႜၸံ

ႜၸံ, ၁ၸံ, ၵ̄ၸံ, တၸံ, ႜ̇ၸံ, ၽိၸံ, ၸ̇ၸံ, ၵ̇ၸံ,
တ̇ၵ̇ ႜၸံ ၵုၸံ̌ ၵ̇Ḱ, ႜၸံ ၁̄ၸ̌ ၵ̇Ḱ. ႜၸံ ၵုR
တ̇ၸ̌, ႜၸံ ၵုR ႜႃ. ၸ̈ၵ̌ ၵၤ ၸ̈Ḱ ၵုၸ̌ ၵ̇R ၸႃ
ၸ̈Ḱ ၸ̇ႃ တ̇ႃ. ၸ̈Ḱ ၵ̇ႃ ၵ̇R ၵၵ̌ ၸ̈Ḱ ၸ̇ႃ ႃ႒
၁ၖ. ႜႃ ၸ̇ၸ̌ ၸႃ̌ ၁ၵ̌ ၵ̇Ḱ တ̇Ḱ ၵၸ̇ ၵၤA.

37

ꩫ꩜

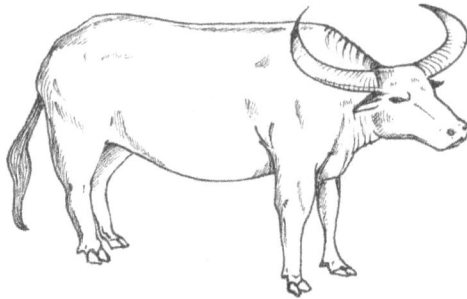

�0ꩫ꩜

ꩡ ꩫ꩜ = ꩡꩫ꩜

38

A

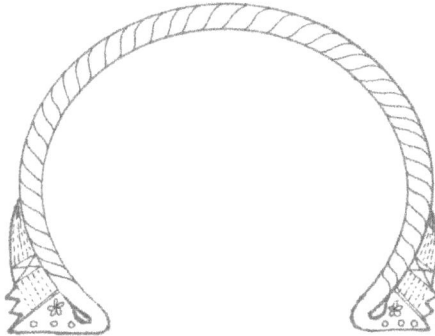

ⵍA

ⵍ   A = ⵍA

ⵍA, ⵀA, ⵇA, ⵋA, ⵃA, ⴺA, ⵟA, ⴲA,
�008A, ⵣA. ⵃⵀⵍA ⵙⵎ ∨ⴰ, ⵃⵀⵍA ⵟK.
ⵀR ⵋA ⵏR ⴷA ⵃⵀⵍA ⵟⵙ ⵊⵋ ⵟⵙ ⵟⵙ.
ⵟⴷ ⵍⵎ ⵍ∀ ⵋⴲ ⵎ∀ⵍA ⵏR ⴷⵙ HR ⵎⴷ
ⵍⵀ ⵟⵘ ⴲⵙ ⵃⵙ.

Ꭺ

ᏩᎧ

Ꮹ Ꭺ = ᏩᎧ

ᏩᎧ, ᎦᎧ, ᎭᎧ, ᎹᎧ, ᎤᎧ, ᏖᎧ, ᏙᎧ, ᎠᎧ.
ᎧᏫᏩᎧ, ᏩᎧᎷᏏ, ᏩᎧᎩᎲ. ᏔᏒᎥᏒᎮᏒ
ᏙᎧᏉᏫᏩᎧ. ᏗᎤᎭᎧ ᏩᎧᎧᏒᎹᏒ ᎤᎯᎤᏫ
ᎫᎤ. ᏗᎤ ᎹᏒᎥᎧᏉᏫᏩᎧᎤᏫᏙᎧᎥᎪ.
ᎤᎤ ᎧᏫᎽᏯᏩᎧᏴᎪᎯ.

40

Ǎ

ᰖᰫǍ

ᰖᰫ Ǎ = ᰖᰫǍ

ᰖᰫǍ, ᰜᰫǍ, ᰝᰫǍ, ᰨǍ, ᰩᰫǍ, ᰘǍ, ᰪǍ, ᰗǍ,
ᰫǍ, ᰜᰫǍ, ᰖᰫǍ, ᰖᰫǍᰝᰨᰩᰫ, ᰖᰫǍᰝᰖᰫᰘ.
ᰨǍᰘᰫᰪǍᰝᰫǍᰝᰨᰖᰫᰜRᰫRᰝᰫǍᰖᰫǍ
ᰛᰗᰕ. ᰪǍᰝᰫǍᰘᰫᰖᰫǍᰝᰫǍᰕ.

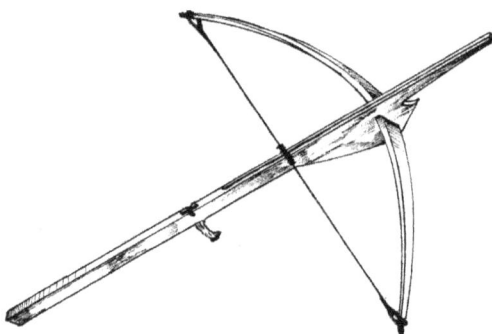

ꓔꙨ

ꓔ Ꙩ = ꓔꙨ

ꓔꙨ, ꓴꙨ, ꓱꙨ, ꙨꙨ, ꓵꙨ, ꓕꙨ, ꓳꙨ, ꓲꙨ,
ꙨꙨ. ꓴꓯꓔꙨ, ꓔꙨꙎꙨꓴꙆꙡ, ꓔꙨꙎꙨꙍꓯ.
ꓴꙨꓵ̄ꓣꙏꙆꓔꙨꓴꙆꙡ. ꓵꙨꓵ̄ꓣꙏꙆꓔꙨ
ꙍꓯ. ꓵꙨꓲꙨꓴꙨꙆꓔꙎꙍꓯꓵꙨꙏꙨ.

43

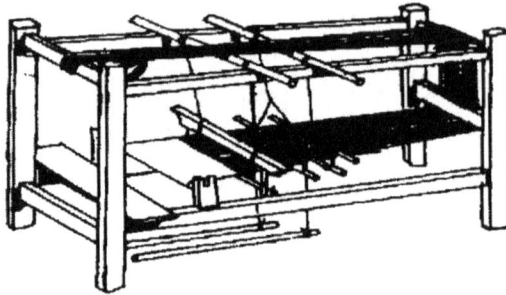

44

4

ᶮᴴ

ᶮ ᴴ = ᶮᴴ

ᄔ

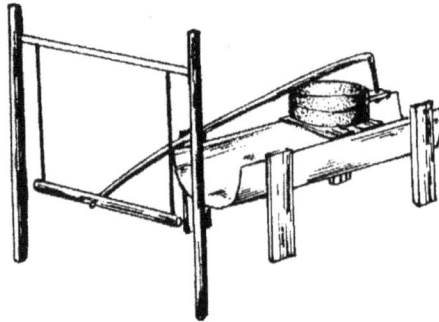

Ⴆᄔ

Ⴆ ᄔ = Ⴆᄔ

Ⴆᄔ, ᠕ᄔ, ᚊᄔ, ᄐᄔ, ᠗ᄔ, ᚖᄔ, ᠋ᄔ, ᛒᄔ.
ᚆᚆႦᄔᚖᄔ᠕Kᛆ, Ⴆᄔᚖᄔᚖᆀᚔᚌ. ᚖᄔ
ᚔᆀ᠋ᚏRᚙᚘᚆᚆႦᄔ. ᛆᚆᛁᚆᚋᆀᚊᚏR
ᚖᄔᚖᆀ. ᛆᚆᚏRᚖᄔ᠋ᄔᚋᄔᚖᆀᚙᚘᛒᚍ.

ﾝ

ﾝﾝ

ﾝ ﾝ = ﾝﾝ

ﾝﾝ, ﾝﾝ, ﾝﾝ, ﾝﾝ, ﾝﾝ, ﾝﾝ, ﾝﾝ, ﾝﾝ.
ﾝﾝﾝﾝﾝﾝﾝﾝ, ﾝﾝﾝﾝﾝﾝ. ﾝﾝﾝﾝﾝﾝ
ﾝﾝﾝRﾝﾝﾝﾝﾝﾝﾝﾝ. ﾝﾝﾝKﾝﾝﾝﾝ
ﾝRﾝﾝﾝﾝﾝﾝ.

n

ຕກ

ຕ ກ = ຕກ

ຕກ, ຕກ, ບກ, ລກ, ວກ, ກກ, ກກ, ບກ,
ວກ. ບກຕກ ∨ຣ໋ ວ, ຕກ ວ໋, ຕກບກ.
ວກ ∨ ∀ ຕຣ ∧໋ ບກ ຕກ ∨ຣ໋ ວ. ກບ ກR
ບບ ກບ ບກ ຕກ ວ໋ ຕ ໋ ຍ໋ ວ໋. ກບ ກR
ບບ ກບ ບກ ຕກ ∨ຣ໋ ວ ຕ ໋ ຍ໋ ກ໋.

48

ພັດ

ພັດ

ພ ັ = ພັດ

ພັດ, ຜັດ, ວັດ, ລັດ, ບັດ, ຫັດ, ພັດ, ກັດ.
ວຍພັດ ກັດ ຝ∧, ພັດ ກັດ ກິຕ. ຫR ກັດ
ມກ ຫR ລັກ ກຕ ກR ຜR ພັດ ທຈ ກ໋. ຫR
ກຸ ກR ລັດ ວບ ກຂ ຜຫ ພັດ ຍ∧ຯ.
ວບ ກຂ ລR ພັດ ວັດຯ.

ກ໌

ເຍ໌

ເຍ ໌ = ເຍ໌

ເຍ໌, ຜ່ຍ໌, ງຍ໌, ລໍຍ໌, ຕິຍ໌, ພຍ໌, ເຍຍ໌, ກໍຍ໌.
ວຍ ຕໍ ເຍ໌, ຕໍ ເຍ໌ ຕິ໌, ຕໍ ເຍ໌ ຍໍ.
ວຍ ຕໍ ເຍ໌ ຍວ ຫໍ. ລ໌ຍຍ ຍR ຕິ໌ ຕໍ
ເຍ໌. ລໍ໌ ຄR ລ໌ ຕິ໌ ຕິຫ ຫE ຕໍ ເຍ໌.
ລໍ໌ ຄR ລ໌ ຕິ໌ ຕິ໌ ພຍ໌ ລ໌ຍຍ.

Ʊ

ꞟU

꜔ ꞟ = ꞟU

ꞟU, ꞟU, ꞟU, ꞟU, ꞟU, ꞟU, ꞟU, ꞟU,
ꞟU, ꞟU ꞟU, ꞟU ꞟU, ꞟU ꞟU, ꞟU ꞟU,
ꞟU ꞟU. ꞟU ꞟU ꞟR ꞟU ꞟU ꞟU ꞟU ꞟU.
ꞟU ꞟU ꞟU ꞟU ꞟU ꞟU ꞟR ꞟU ꞟU ꞟU
ꞟU ꞟU.

ᱯ

ᱞᱯ

ᱞ ᱯ = ᱞᱯ

ᱞᱯ, ᱯᱯ, ᱬᱯ, ᱠᱯ, ᱢᱯ, ᱴᱯ, ᱨᱯ, ᱡᱯ,
ᱞᱯ ᱰᱟ, ᱞᱯ ᱨᱨ, ᱞᱯ ᱶᱦᱭ, ᱞᱯ ᱞK.
ᱜᱚᱢ ᱞᱯ ᱞK ᱴᱦ ᱴᱦ ᱠᱟ ᱚᱪ ᱚᱡ ᱭᱟ.
ᱞᱯ ᱯᱭ ᱢᱢ ᱴᱢ ᱚᱫ ᱚᱦ ᱡK ᱚᱡ.

บ้

ตบ้

ต บ้ = ตบ้

ตบ้, ลบ้, ปบ้, ฌบ้. ฅอ้ ตบ้ มห ต่ภ, ตบ้ ต้อ้ มพ้. ตบ้ ม่A้ ห ตบ ฆ้V พK ลอ้. ตบ้ พห ฌR ฆ้V พR ป ภ ตบ ปบ้ ฆ้ะ. หR ฆA ฆบ้ห พบ้ ตบ้.

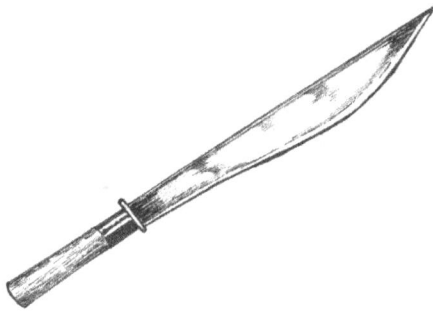

ꤵꤪ

ꤵ ꤪ = ꤵꤪ

ꤵꤪ, ꤜꤪ, ꤢꤪ, ꤔꤪ, ꤕꤪ, ꤠꤪ, ꤟꤪ, ꤝꤪ,
ꤓꤪ, ꤚꤪ, ꤜꤪ. ꤢꤪꤵꤪ, ꤵꤪꤖꤚ꤬ꤖꤲK, ꤵꤪ
ꤢꤲꤜꤰ꤬. ꤞꤪꤛRꤢꤩ꤬ꤵꤪꤢꤲꤜꤰ꤬. ꤢ꤬ꤛR
ꤢꤩ꤬ꤵꤪꤖꤚ꤬ꤖꤲK. ꤞꤪꤨꤰ꤬ ꤢ꤬ ꤏꤛ ꤟꤲꤛR
ꤢꤩ꤬ꤵꤪꤢ꤯ꤗꤰ꤬ꤗꤲ ꤠꤟ꤬ꤢꤩ꤬ꤝꤲ.

54

ံ

ဃံဗံ

ဃံ ဗံ = ဃံဗံ

ဃံဗံ, ဟဗံ, တဗံ, လဗံ, ၬဗံ, ၭဗံ, ၰဗံ, ၪဗံ.
တဂံဃံဗံဃၬှဲၰၭ, ဃံဗံၰၬၬှဲ ၰၬှဲ. ဟဟၮၮ
ၰၭလၭှဲၮၭှဲဃံဗံလၭှဲၰဗံၰၭၟ ၟှဲလၭှဲ, လၰ
လၭှဲၰဗံၰၭၟ ၟှဲ ဟၮ. တၭှဲတၟှဲၰဗံၬၭှဲ.

55

ㅂ

ㅂ = ㅂ

ㅂ, ᄉㅂ, ᄒㅂ, ᄆㅂ, ᄎㅂ, ᄀㅂ, ᄂㅂ, ᄋㅂ.
ᄊᄊㅂᄌᄋ, ㅂᄒ, ㅂᄅᄇᄂ, ㅂᄎ
ᄉR. ᄆᄋᄒᄌᄉᄍᄒWRㅂᄅᄇᄂᄁ
ㅂᄎᄉRᄊᄒ. ᄀᄋᄉRᄌᄆᄆᄉᄂR
ᄊㅂWR.

M

ա‍M

ա‍ M = ա‍M

ա‍M, та̄M, тᴎ, а̇ᴎ, ᴦᴎ, а̇ᴎ, ᴨᴎ, ᴘᴎ.
ᴦա‍Mа̇Ǩ‍ᴡа̇̇, а̄ᴎа‍Mᴥᴀ̇ а̇∀. а̄ᴎта̇ա‍M
а̄ᴎта̇а̇Ǩ‍ᴡа̇̇. ᴧа̇̇ᴧᴀ̇̇ա‍Mᴧᴀ̇̇а̇Ǩᴘа̇̇
а̇̇а̇̇. ᴧа̇̇ᴧᴋ̇а̇а̇̇ᴧа̇̇а̇∀ᴎа̇ᴥᴀ̇ а̇∀.

ЄӢМ

ЄӢ Ӎ = ЄӢМ

ЄӢМ, ЄӢМ, ѠМ, ѢМ, ѺМ, ѶМ, ҤМ, ѳМ.
ѦѽЄӢМ, ЄӢМѢҔ, ЄӢМѽҲ, ЄӢМѳҼ.
ѽҲ ѦЄѝ, ѦRЄӢМ ѳҼ ЄӢМѽҲ ѹҶҦK
ҔAЛA. ҤѮ ѽѮ ѽK, ѦRЄӢМ ѳҼ ЄӢМѽҲ
ѳҶѝѝ Лѕ.

58

М̌

ᴧМ̌

ᴧ М̌ = ᴧМ̌

ᴧМ̌, �☉М̌, ᴐМ̌, ᴨМ̌, ᴐМ̌. ᴧМ̌ᴆᴕ̌, ᴧМ̌ᴇᴪ.
ᴨᴈ̌ ᴧМ̌ᴆᴕ̌ ᴧ☉М̌ ᴐМ̌ ᴧ☉М̌ ᴐМ̌. ᴨᴈ̌ ᴧМ̌ᴆᴕ̌
ᴧ☉М̌ᴆᴎ ᴈᴧ. ᴧᴿ ᴧᴧ ᴨᴈ̌ᴕᴧ ᴧᴧ ᴆᴕ̌ᴨᴿ
ᴆᴛᴆᴈᴆᴪ ᴧМ̌ᴆᴕ̌ ᴫᴌ.

ຟືນ

ຟື ນ = ຟືນ

ຟືນ, ສນ, ບໍນ, ຫນ, ພນ. ຟືນບໍ້, ຫຍິງຫ້
ຟືນ, ແຕຍຫ້ຟືນ. ຫຍິງຫ້ຟືນບໍ້ຍໍມຫ.
ແຕຍຫ້ຟືນບໍ້ຫໍມຫໍ. ແຫຫີຈຫໍນຫໍ
ຫໍໝໍ້ບໍຟືນບໍໍຫໍນໍໝໍ.

60

ꭰ̇

Ꮘꭰ̇

Ꮟ ꭰ̇ = Ꮘꭰ̇

Ꮘꭰ̇, Ꮹꭰ̇, ꮿꭰ̇, ꭹꭰ̇, ꭶꭰ̇, ꮽꭰ̇, Ꮫꭰ̇, ꭾꭰ̇
ꮵꮧᏈꭰ̇, Ꮘꭰ̇ꭲꮄ, Ꮘꭰ̇ꮖꮄ. ᏤᎡꮝꮅꭰ́Ꭾ
ꮃꮧꭿᏈꭰ̇. ᏤᎡꮝ�ꭿ ꮑꮽꭿꮄꭾꮧᎮ
ꮦꭰ̇ꮵꮅᏔA.

61

ᎳᎦ̌

Ꮃ Ꭰ̌ = ᎳᎦ̌

ᎳᎦ̌, ᎧᎦ̌, �Ꭶ̌, Ꭳ̄Ꭰ̌, ᎫᎦ̌, ᎬᎦ̌, ᎶᎦ̌, ᎤᎦ̌.
Ꭲ̄ᎳᎦ̌, ᎶRᎳᎦ̌, ᎳᎳᎳᎦ̌, Ꭳ̄Ꮃ ᎳᎦ̌, ᎾR̄
ᎳᎦ̌, ᎤᎬᎳᎦ̌. ᎶᎳᎧᎬ ᎤᎦ̌ Ꭳ̄Ꭰ̌ᎶᎳ ᎾᎳ ᎿᎳ
ᎤᎬᎳᎦ̌ᎫᎸᎺᎼᎭ. ᎳᎦ̌ᎶᎦ̌Ꭽ, ᎳᎦ̌ᎳᎸᎶᎦ̌.

E

ɅE

Ʌ E = ɅE

ɅE, ЊE, ȦE, ՈE, ʌE, ŴE, ꟽE, ƎE.
ƏV ɅE, ɅE Ȧk, ɅE Ə, ɅE ŴE.
ɱḱ ɅE ƎṀ ՈK, ɅE ƎṀ ŴE. ȞȞ ʌE Jṁ
ʋṁ ĀR ȞV ɅE. ШШ ĀV ȞȞ ẇE ʋṁ ĀR
ṅ ɅE ĀV ЊШ ẏȞ ȞK.

Ė

∩Ė

∩ Ė = ∩Ė

∩Ė, ℧Ė, ⍩Ė, ⅃Ė, ⅊Ė. ⍥∩Ė, ∩Ė ⅀⍨, ∩Ė ⍩R, ∩Ė ⍥⍜. ℧⍨ ℧ ℧ ∩Ė ⍵⍨ ℧Ė⍗. ⋁⍨ ℧⍜ ∩Ė ⍵⍨ ⍩R⅃Ė⍗. ⍵⍜ ⍵Ė ⍥⍜ ⍩ ⅃Ė. ⍥⍨ ℧⍨ ℧R⍗ ∩Ė ⅀⍨.

Ĕ

ὐĔ

ὐ Ĕ = ὐĔ

ὐĔ, ʁĔ, Ɔ̆Ĕ, ʚ̆Ĕ, ὐ̈Ĕ. ∩Ʒ̆ὐĔ, ὐĔ∩ᴋ,
ὐĔὐ̇Ř, ὐĔ」ᴨ. ὐ̈Ĕ∇Ʒ̆ ᴫ⊓̇ʚᴜ ὐĔ ∩Ř
⊙Ч ⍵̈Ч⅄Ʒ̆ ᴍᴨ ᴕЧ. ὐĔʚᴨ ⊙Ʒ̆ ʁĔ ⍵̈Ʒ̆
ᴔᴨ ᴓᴀᴕЧ. ʁĔ ᴔ∀⊙K̇ ʚᴜ ὐĔ ⍵Ʒ̆.

ထံဟ

ထံ ဟ = ထံဟ

ထံဟ, ဃဟ, �, ဃၵဟ. ကၟံ ထံဟ, ထံဟ ၉ဒၟံ, ထံဟ
ၥံၯ ၶဃ. ဃၯၵၮၟံ ဃၟံ ၵၯ ကၟံ ထံဟ ၥံၯ ၶဃ
ၐၵၯၵ ၯၷ ၯၵၯၯ ၔၯ ထံဟ ၯၵ ၯၟံ ၵၟံ ၓၯၵၯံ.

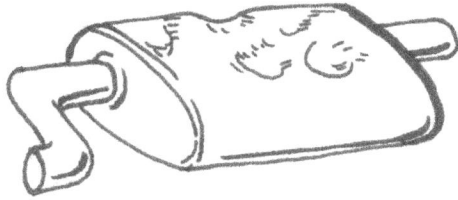

ꪶꪚꪲ

ꪶꪚꪲ   ꪶꪚꪲ = ꪶꪚꪲ

ꤵꤢ̌

ꤞꤢꤵꤢ̌

ꤞꤢ ꤵꤢ̌ = ꤞꤢꤵꤢ̌

꤮ꤢꤵꤢ̌ ꤞꤢꤵꤢ̌, ꤕꤢꤵꤢ̌ ꤟꤢꤵꤢ̌, ꤮ꤢꤵꤢ̌, ꤟꤢꤵꤢ̌. ꤢꤢꤟꤢꤪ ꤮ꤢꤵꤢ̌ ꤞꤢꤵꤢ̌. ꤝꤢ ꤟꤢꤪ ꤕꤢꤵꤢ̌ ꤠꤢꤵꤢ̌. ꤟꤢꤟꤢ ꤝꤢꤪ ꤢꤢꤟꤢꤪ ꤮ꤢꤵꤢ̌ ꤞꤢꤵꤢ̌ ꤛꤢ ꤟꤢꤪ ꤟꤢꤢ ꤣꤢꤟ. ꤟꤢꤟꤢ ꤝꤢ ꤝꤢ ꤟꤢꤵꤢ̌ ꤟꤢꤵꤢ̌ ꤕꤢꤵꤢ̌ ꤠꤢꤵꤢ̌ ꤥꤢꤪ ꤛꤢ ꤟꤢ ꤣꤢꤟ.

ᨵᨦ

ᨵᨩᨦ

$$ᨵᨩ \; ᨦ = ᨵᨩᨦ$$

ᨵᨩᨦ, ᨩᨦ. ᨴᨳᨩᨦ ᨦᨷ ᨵᨩᨦᨠᨰ ᨧᨩᨦᨧᨠ ᨵᨩᨦ?. ᨵᨠᨵᨩᨦᨠᨰ ᨩᨠᨵᨩᨵᨵᨩᨦ. ᨦᨷ ᨰᨰ ᨵᨩᨦᨵᨠᨵᨵᨩᨲᨵᨩᨵᨵᨵᨩᨵ ᨵᨩᨦ?. ᨵᨠ ᨰᨰᨵᨩᨦ ᨵᨵ ᨵᨩᨦ.

ႃ

ဖ�ာႆ

ဖ ာႆ = ဖႆ

ဖႆ. ကဖႆ, ဒိဖႆ. ကဖႆ ပိဟံ ဃၢႆ ဧၢႆ.
ကၢၢ် လၢၢ် ဖႆ ပိဟံ. လၢၢ် ဖႆ ပိဟံ ဟၢၢ က．

70

ဋ̌

ဈ ̌

ဈ ̌ = ဈ ̌

ᤐᤢᤱᤖᤫᤠᤳ

ᤅᤖᤕᤠ ᤐᤤᤒᤤ, ᤕᤠ ᤀᤖ ᤌᤧᤶᤔ ᤤᤠᤕᤠ ᤔᤣᤶ ᤒᤤᤒ
ᤀᤠᤐᤖ ᤝᤧ ᤝᤕᤠᤏᤧᤶ ᤌᤜᤫᤠᤠ ᤅᤖ ᤜᤤᤗᤗᤤ, ᤍᤤ
ᤝᤕᤕᤠᤕ ᤐᤥᤀ ᤏᤢ ᤊᤓᤠ ᤐᤤᤒᤤ ᤔᤣᤶ ᤊᤓᤠ ᤐᤤᤒ ᤔᤣᤶᤏᤧᤶ
ᤊᤓᤠ ᤐᤤᤒ ᤀᤖ ᤌᤧᤠᤏᤧᤶ ᤜᤤᤗᤗᤤ.

ᤒᤜ	ᤌᤒ	ᤀᤠᤃ
ᤐᤤᤒ	ᤜᤤᤗᤤ	ᤈᤠᤠ
ᤃᤠᤴ	ᤌᤀ	ᤐᤱ
ᤛᤗ	ᤄᤧᤛᤤ	ᤏᤧᤶ

1      _____   _____

2      _____   _____

3      _____   _____

4      _____   _____

5   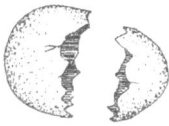   _____   _____

6      _____   _____

7  _____ _____

8  _____ _____

9 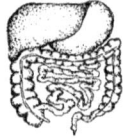 _____ _____

10  _____ _____

11  _____ _____

12  _____ _____

ꤚꓤ̇ �73️ꓤ̇R

1, ꤛ ꤿ . ꤿ .

2, ꤿ . ꤿ .

3, ꤿ . ꤿ
ꤿ .

4, ꤿ , ꤿ . ꤿ , ꤿ .

5, ꤿ , ꓤR ꤿ . ꤿ
ꓤR ꤿ .

6, ꤿ , ꓤR ꤿ . ꤿ ,
ꓤR ꤿ .

7, ꤿ . ꤿ
.

8, ꤿ ,
ꤿ .

9, ꤿ . ꤿ
ꤿ .

10, ꤿ , ꤿ .

11, ꤿ , ꤿ . ꤿ , ꤿ
ꤿ .

75

ᤁᤡᤔ ᤂᤧᤰ ᤕᤢᤰ

1, ...

2, ...

3, ...

4, ...

5, ...

6, ...

7, ...

8, ...

9, ...

10, ᐱᐦᒦ ᐅᒪᒍ ᐅᒥ ᑖᖘ ᐱᐦᒦ ᓅᖠᖚ ᖢᒫᔑᓇ. ᐱᐦᒦ ᐅᒪᒣᖛᐸ ᑖᖘ ᐱᐦᒦ ᓅᖠ ᑛᖝ ᖢᒪ.

11, ᐱᐦᒦ ᐅᒪᐊ ᐣᔑ, ᑖᖘ ᐱᐦᒦ ᓅᖠᓅᒉ ᐅᒧ. ᐱᐦᒦ ᐅᒪᐊᑎᖘ, ᑖᖘ ᐱᐦᒦ ᓅᖠ ᐠᒉᒣᐠ, ᐱᐦᒦ ᐣᒣ ᔪᒧ ᒎᒉᖟᐠ ᑖᖘ ᐱᐦᒦ ᓅᖠ ᑛᖝ ᒣᖑ ᒡᖛ ᖫᒪ ᒍᒦ ᖢᒨᖠᐠ ᐣᒨ ᖢᒦ ᖢᒨ.

12, ᖬᖔᒉᖤ ᒎᒉ ᖫᖑᖢᒦ. ᖠᐠ ᒉᒦᒎᐠ ᖣᐁ ᒎᒉ ᖫᖑᖢᒪ. ᖬᒎᒉᖬᒦ ᖬᖘ ᒣᒫ ᖢᒉ ᑦᖑ ᐣᒨ ᖢᒦ ᖬᒎᒉ ᖢᒦ ᖢᒦ ᖫᒫᖘ ᖬᒎ ᐣᒨ ᖢᒦ ᖤᐠ ᖬᒉ ᐣᖘ ᖫᖑ ᖬᖘ ᑦᖢ ᒣᒫ ᖢᒉ ᑦᖑ ᐣᒨ ᖢᒦ ᖢᒦ.

13, ᖬᒦᒉᖤ ᖢᒨᖨᖢᒫ, ᖢᒫ ᖪᐠ ᒎᒫ ᖬᒦᒉᖤ ᖢᒨᖢᒫ, ᖬᒦ ᑦᐱᖠᐁ, ᖢᒫ ᖪᐠ ᒎᒫ ᖬᒦ ᑦᐱ ᖢᖤ. ᖣᐁ ᔪᒧ ᖢᐠ ᖬᒦ ᐣᐠ ᖪᐠ ᐣᒉᖣᐁ ᔪᒉ ᖠᐁ. ᖣᐁ ᔪᒧ ᖢᖣᖛ ᖪᐠ ᐣᒉᖣᐁ ᔪᒧ ᖢᐠ.

14, ᖢᖔᖢᒦᖢᒦᖣᒉ, ᒎᒨᓅᒦᖣᒫ ᐣᒧᖣᒉ, ᔪᒧ ᖢᒦᖢᒦ ᖣᐠ ᒎᒨᓅᒦᖣᒫ ᐣᒧᖤᖛ. ᖬᒉ ᖪᐠ ᖣᖢᖠ ᑖᒧ ᖢᒉ ᖫᖣ ᖣᐠ ᖣᐁ ᔪᒧ ᖢᖣᒡᖛ ᖣᐁ ᔪᒧ ᖢᐠ, ᐱᑕ ᖬᒉ ᖪᐠ ᒎᒦ ᖣᐁ ᔪᒧ ᖢᐠ ᒡᖛ ᖣᐁ ᔪᒧ ᖣᐁ ᒣᒫ ᖣᐁ ᖪᒦ.

15, ᖣᒦ ᖢᒦ ᖫᒎᒋᖢᐁ ᒎᐁ, ᖢᖛ ᖬᖔ ᖢᒎᒋᖢᒨ ᒎᖔ. ᖬᒉ ᖪᐠ ᒡᒉᖢᖛ ᖫᖔ ᖪᖛ ᐱᐦᒦ ᖬᐠ ᖫᖔ ᒣᒫ ᖨᖪ ᖬᒉ ᖪᐠ ᒎᒨ.

16, ᖣᒦ ᐱᐦᒦ ᖫᒉ, ᖢᒦ ᐱᐦᒦ ᒡᐠ. ᖪᖢ ᐱᐦᒦ ᖫᖑ, ᐅᐁ ᐱᐦᒦ ᒡᒨ. ᖢᖛ ᒡᒫ ᒉᒦ ᒎᒋᒉᖤ ᖤ ᖫᖣ ᖤ ᖪᒦ ᖬᒉ ᖢᖢ ᖢᖔ ᖘ ᑦᐊ.

ဘျၢ် ထၢ်ဖှၢ်

1, ...

2, ...

3, ...

4, ...

5, ...

6, ...

7, ...

8, ...

9, ...

10, ...

11, ...

12, ...

13, [illegible]

14, [illegible]

15, [illegible]

16, [illegible]

17, [illegible]

18, [illegible]

19, [illegible]

20, [illegible]

21, [illegible]

22, [illegible]

23, [illegible]

24, [illegible]

25,

26,

27,

28,

29,

30,

31,

32,

33,

34,

35,

36,

37,

38,

39,

40,

41,

ꓓ႞ ဃဃ Ⴆဂ

1) R   Ṙ   Ř̌   ꓕR ᴕ̇Ṙ ᚺŘ̌

2) K   K̇   Ǩ   ᚻK ꓕ̇K̇ ᛎǨ

3) ဃ   ဃ̇   ဃ̈   ᐯဃ ᛎ̇ဃ̇ ᚺဃ̈

4) ᅚ   ᅚ̇   ᅚ̈   ᑌᅚ ᛎ̇ᅚ̇ ယᅚ̈

5) ᒪ   ᒪ̇   ᒪ̈   ဃᒪ ᚲ̇ᒪ̇ ᴕᒪ̈

6) ∀   ∀̇   ∀̌   ᴕ∀ ᛎ̇∀̇ ᴕ∀̌

7) ᏟС   Ċ   Č̌   ᐯС ᚺĊ ᛎČ̌

8) ᗰ   ᗰ̇   ᗰ̈   ꓕᗰ ဃᗰ̇ ᗺᗰ̈

9) ꓜ   ꓜ̇   ꓜ̈   ᕮꓜ ꓴꓜ̇ ᚻꓜ̈

10) A   Ȧ   Ǎ   ꓴA ᛎȦ ᚺǍ

11)

12)

13)

14)

15)

16)

17)

18)

19)

20)

Ꞙยꞛ

ยꞘꞌ ꞚꞠꞝRꞙꞛ

ยꞘꞌ ꞚꞠ ꞝR ꞙꞛ........ꞛꞛ ꞥꞠ ꞙ........ꞥ ꞣꞚ ꞥꞤ
ꞘꞠ ꞠꞠ ꞣꞙ ꞥꞥ........ยꞘꞌ ꞘꞤ ꞣꞚ........ꞙꞥ ꞥꞛ ยꞘꞌ ꞣꞥ
ꞣꞠ ꞥ ꞝ ꞥꞛ........ꞙꞣꞚ ꞝ ꞥꞥ ꞙꞤ
ꞝ ꞣꞠ ꞝ ꞥꞛ........ꞝ ꞙꞣ Ꞙꞥ ꞙꞣ ꞛꞚ

ꞣꞠ ยꞘꞌ ꞚꞠ ꞛ........ꞛꞛ ꞥ ꞥꞤ........ꞣꞙ ꞣꞚ ꞙꞣ
ꞛꞛ ꞥ ꞠR Ꞙꞥ........ꞙꞣꞚ ꞝ ꞣ ꞣꞚ ꞣ ꞝꞚ
ꞣꞤ Ꞡꞣ ꞣꞥ ꞙꞥ........ꞛꞛ ꞙꞣ ꞙꞣ ꞣꞥ ꞥꞥ
ꞙꞣ ꞙꞣ ꞣꞥ ꞥꞣ........ꞝ ꞣ ꞝ ꞥꞚ...

꞊ꞣꞥ ꞝꞥ ꞝ........꞊ꞣꞥ ꞣ ꞥꞙ ꞣ ꞥꞤ
ยꞘꞌ ꞙꞛ ꞥꞙ........꞊ꞣꞣ ꞣꞣ ꞥꞙ
ꞣ ꞛꞥ ꞥꞙ........ꞠR ꞣꞥ ꞥꞙ
ꞣꞣ ꞝꞥ ꞙꞛ........ꞙꞣ Ꞙꞥ ꞥꞣ

ꞡꞤ ꞣꞥ ꞙꞣ꞊ ꞛ........ꞠR ꞣꞙ ꞙꞠR
ꞛꞛ ꞥꞙ ꞣꞣ ꞝꞥ........ꞥꞙ ꞣꞥ ꞣꞙ ꞝꞣ
꞊ꞙꞛ ꞣꞙ ꞝꞤ........ꞙꞠR ꞣꞙ ꞙꞠR ꞥꞤ
Ꞙꞛ ꞙꞥ ꞣꞠ ꞥꞣ........ꞥꞙ ꞣꞥ ꞙꞠR ꞣꞥ ꞛꞥ
꞊ꞣꞥ ꞙꞥ ꞠꞠ ꞛꞥ........ꞥꞙ ꞣꞥ ꞥꞙ ꞣꞥ....

ᥥᐱ ᐺᖋ ᙈᐞ

ᥬᖋ ᥰᙈ ᥤᒄ ᨉᱷ ᥰᑊ ᥰᥰ ᥰᖋ ᙈᱷ ᥰᖋᥤᒄ ᥰᖋ ᥧᖋ
ᥧᖋ ᖋᥴᥰᥰᥐR ᥰ, ᙈᥬ ᥰᖋ ᨉᖋ ᖋᥐ ᥤᖋ ᨉR ᥰ ᥧᖋ.

ᖋᥰ ᖋᕠ ᖋ ᥧᖋ ᒄᥰ ᥬᖋ ᥐᙰ

(signature)

ᑊ ᖋᥰ ᙈᖋ ᥰᕠ ᖋᥴ ᥰᙈ ᥰ

ᥰᙈ ᐺᖋ ᐺᖋ

ᖋᥰ ᐺᖋ ᙈᐞ: ᖋᥴ ᥰᙈ ᥰ
ᥥᱷ ᖋᖋ ᥰᕠ: ᖋᥴ ᥤᥴ ᖋᥬ
ᖋᥰ ᙈᖋ ᥰᖋ: ᖋᥴ ᙈᥬ ᖋᥰ

ᥥᖋ ᥬᙈ ᥤᒄ ᙈᐞ ᨉᙈ ᥰᕠ ᖋA ᥥᖋ ᙈR ᙈᥰ ᥥA ᥰᖋ
ᥤᕠ ᥰᥰ ᥴᥴ ᖋᕠ 5 / 5 / [1995. ᥤᙈ ᥰᥰ ᥴᥰ
ᥤᕠ ᥰᥰ ᥴᥴ: 5 / 11 / 1999. ᥤᙈ ᥰᥰ ᥴᥰ
ᥤᕠ ᥰᥰ ᥴᥴ: 8 / 4 / 2009

* 9 7 8 1 6 2 2 3 5 0 0 8 7 *